Abe Lincoln

THE YOUNG YEARS

Abe Lincoln

THE YOUNG YEARS

by Keith Brandt
illustrated by John Lawn

Troll Associates

Library of Congress Cataloging in Publication Data

Brandt, Keith (date)
   Abe Lincoln, the young years.

    Summary: Focuses on events from Abraham Lincoln's
youth in Kentucky and Indiana which proved influen-
tial in his later life.
    1. Lincoln, Abraham, 1809-1865—Childhood and
youth—Juvenile literature.   2. Presidents—United
States—Biography—Juvenile literature. [1. Lincoln,
Abraham, 1809-1865. 2. Presidents] I. Lawn,
John, ill. II. Title.
E457.32.B79   973.7′092′4 [B] [92]   81-23172
ISBN 0-89375-750-0   AACR2
ISBN 0-89375-751-9 (pbk)

Abe Lincoln

THE YOUNG YEARS

The sun was just starting to push its way over the horizon. Its golden light chased away the shadows of the woods around the cabin at Sinking Springs Farm. But the air stayed chilly and cold this morning of February 12, 1809, as it almost always does during a Kentucky winter.

It was nearly as cold inside the one-room log cabin. But the people in the room were too busy to care about that. Mr. Tom Lincoln sat on a chair in one corner, talking quietly to Sarah, his two-year-old daughter.

"Your mother will be just fine," he said. "You sit right here on pappy's lap and don't worry about a thing."

A few moments later, the loud wail of a baby was heard.

"It's a boy, Tom," Elizabeth Sparrow called out. Elizabeth, Mrs. Nancy Lincoln's aunt, had come to the cabin the day before to help with the birth.

The infant, named Abraham after his grandfather, had a strong voice. He was a large baby, sturdy and healthy looking. But he was very homely. At least, that was what nine-year-old Dennis Hanks thought. Dennis, the Sparrows' adopted son, came to see his new cousin as soon as the adults would let him into the cabin.

Dennis would always remember the day Abraham Lincoln was born. When he entered the cabin, Dennis saw Nancy Lincoln lying in bed, looking tired, but very happy. Tom Lincoln threw a bearskin over Nancy to keep her warm, and then he built a great fire.

Betsy Sparrow was busy washing and dressing the new baby. Dennis asked if he could hold little Abe. Nancy said, "Yes, but be careful," and handed him the squirming infant.

As soon as Abe was in his cousin's arms, he began to wail. The more Dennis tried to soothe him, the louder Abe cried. At last, Dennis handed the baby back to Mrs. Sparrow. "Take him!" Dennis said. "He'll never amount to much."

Sinking Springs Farm was Abe's home for the first two years of his life. Then Tom Lincoln got tired of trying to grow crops in poor, rocky soil. So he moved his family to a farm at Knob Creek, ten miles away. As soon as they got there, Mr. Lincoln, a skilled carpenter, set to work building a log cabin and furniture.

It was easier for the pioneers to make new furniture than to carry old furniture from one place to another. Once they settled in a new place, they had to cut down many trees to clear the land for farming. That gave them a great amount of wood to build a cabin, furniture, and fences, and still have plenty left over for firewood.

Like most pioneer children, Abe and Sarah helped with the chores. Once he was big enough, Abe cleaned ashes from the fireplace. He filled the woodbox with dry branches that he collected in the forest. He hauled water from the creek. And he did anything else his mother or father asked him to do. Sarah helped her mother tend the farm animals, do the cooking and baking, wash the clothes, and tidy the cabin.

Abe's earliest memories of childhood were of those days at Knob Creek. "I remember very well," he wrote, "our farm was composed of three fields. It lay in the valley surrounded by high hills and deep gorges. Sometimes when there came a big rain in the hills, the water would come down through the gorges and spread all over the farm....I remember one Saturday afternoon. We planted pumpkin and corn seeds in what we called the big field; it contained seven acres—and I dropped the pumpkin seed. I dropped two seeds every other hill and every other row. The next Sunday morning there came a big rain in the hills; it did not rain a drop in the valley, but the water coming down through the gorges washed ground, corn, pumpkin seeds, and all clear off the field."

Life was a struggle for frontier families like the Lincolns. They needed every bit of food they could grow to feed themselves through the year.

One long dry spell or one bad flood could destroy a whole year's crops. And if that happened, it brought terrible hardship to the farm families. They barely stayed alive, eating berries and nuts from the forest, and any game they could hunt. It was tough enough to live this way in warm weather, but it could mean starving in the winter.

The flood that Abe never forgot didn't cause too much suffering. That is because it came so early in the planting season. This gave the Lincolns enough time to plant another crop. So Abe and his father, along with Mr. Sparrow and Dennis Hanks, worked from morning till night, reseeding the field.

Life wasn't all work for little Abe. He spent lots of time exploring the woods, fishing in the creek, and hunting with his father and the dogs.

There were many exciting things to do for a young boy growing up in Kentucky. But there was danger, too. One Sunday, Abe was out playing with his best friend, Austin Gollaher.

The boys wanted to cross Knob Creek to find some partridges they had spotted the day before. Rain had made the creek's waters deep and dangerous. But that didn't stop the boys.

There was only one way to cross the creek. That was to walk across a log that stretched from one side to the other. Abe went first, and fell in halfway across. "Neither of us could swim," Austin recalled. "I got a long pole and held it out to Abe, who grabbed it. Then I pulled him ashore. He was almost dead, and I was badly scared." Austin rolled and pounded Abe. Then he shook him, until the water came pouring out of his mouth. Abe was finally all right, and the two friends sat on the creek bank, talking about Abe's narrow escape.

Nancy Hanks Lincoln knew there were many dangers in the forest, and she was strict with her little boy when she had to be. But most of the time she was sweet and gentle and loving. She wanted only the best for her children. So, when a school was opened down the road, Abe and Sarah were enrolled.

Zachariah Riney's one-room schoolhouse was a two-mile walk from the Lincoln homestead. It was a log cabin with a dirt floor and rows of rough log desks and benches. Mr. Riney taught "reading, writing, and ciphering," and he kept order with a birch rod.

The pupils said their lessons out loud, even their arithmetic. It sounded noisy and confused, which is why this kind of school was called a "blab school." The children learned their ABC's, how to spell a few words, and how to do very simple arithmetic. Six-year-old Abe practiced his letters by writing with a charcoal stick on the flat side of a split log. He wanted to make the letters as well as Mr. Riney made them. So he practiced every chance he got, when he wasn't doing chores.

The school was not free. But the frontier people were too poor to pay for their children's schooling with money. Instead, some paid the teacher with a bushel of corn or potatoes or a smoked ham. Other parents paid with fur skins from animals they had trapped, a cord of firewood, or anything else the teacher was willing to take.

The Lincoln children did not attend Mr. Riney's school for very long. In 1816, when Abe was seven, the Lincolns decided to move from Kentucky to Indiana. And in December of that year, with frost covering the ground, they left Knob Creek forever. They traveled northwest through forests, across the Ohio River, and into Indiana. After a rough journey, they reached their new home in the wilderness at Pigeon Creek.

The first thing the Lincolns did was to build a
shelter. With snow falling steadily, the whole
family worked to put up a kind of shed called a
half-faced camp. It had just three walls made of
logs, and a roof of branches and bark. The
fourth side was left open.

A blazing fire burned day and night at the
open side. During the day, Mrs. Lincoln cooked
over the flames. At night, the fire kept the
family from freezing as they slept on their
"beds"—piles of leaves. All their furniture had
been left behind in Kentucky. Tom planned to
make beds, tables, and chairs as soon as he had
time to build a real cabin. But the very first
thing Tom Lincoln had to do, before beginning
the cabin, was to cut down some trees.

Abe worked alongside his father. It took weeks for the father and son to chop down enough trees for a cabin. There were so many other things to do every day—keep the fire at the camp blazing, fetch water from the spring a mile away, clear the land of stumps and stones to ready it for spring planting, and hunt for game to eat.

The woods were filled with all kinds of wild game. There were deer, bears, wild turkeys, ducks, geese, squirrels, rabbits, and wild pigeons. Years later, Abe remembered the day he shot his first—and only— wild turkey. When he saw he had hit the bird, he felt like a real hunter. He was proud to bring good food to the table. But when he saw the dead bird fall to earth, he felt very sad. From that day on, Abe didn't want to be a hunter. He did not like the idea of killing. This feeling stayed with him for the rest of his life.

The Lincolns' cabin was completed early that spring, and the family was glad to have a real home again. It was just one room, like their Knob Creek home had been, but with one big difference! Mr. Lincoln planned something special for the cabin at Pigeon Creek.

"I reckon you children are about ready to have a place to yourselves," Tom Lincoln told Abe and Sarah. "So I have an idea that I think you'll like."

"What is it?" Abe asked.

"I'm putting an open loft over part of the cabin," Mr. Lincoln said. "And I'm knocking some pegs in the wall so you can climb up there."

The children loved their sleeping loft. The first day, they found countless reasons to climb up and down their ladder of wooden pegs. And when the first harvest was in, and Nancy Lincoln made them new cornhusk beds, Abe and Sarah thought their sleeping loft was the greatest room in the world!

In the fall of 1817, Tom and Betsy Sparrow and Dennis Hanks joined the Lincolns in Indiana. They moved into the half-faced camp Tom had built. The Lincolns were very glad to have their relatives so close. It had been lonely without them, especially with the nearest neighbors miles away.

The happiness didn't last very long. In the summer of 1818, Tom and Betsy Sparrow fell ill. They had "milk sickness." It was caused by drinking milk from cows that had eaten poisonous plants. Nancy nursed her aunt and uncle, but without a doctor or medicine it was hopeless. The Sparrows died in September. Not long after, Nancy became ill, too, and died of the same sickness on October 5, 1818.

The world was a drab and lonely place for the Lincoln family. Sarah did her best to cook and clean, and Abe worked hard with his father and Dennis out in the fields. But the spirit had gone out of all of them. Their clothes grew ragged, and the house got dirtier and dirtier.

Then, in November 1819, Tom Lincoln took a trip back to Kentucky. He told the children to be good and take care of themselves till he got back. He rode off into the woods, promising to return as soon as he could.

It was a frightening time for the youngsters. At night they could hear bears and wildcats prowling in the dark woods near the cabin. During the day things were better. Dennis shot quail and rabbits for dinner. Abe and Sarah gathered nuts and berries in the woods. Abe also ground corn for Sarah to bake into pone cakes. It wasn't easy living this way, but it kept them from thinking too much about their fears and loneliness.

Then one sunny day in December, the children heard the sound of a wagon coming through the woods. They ran out of the house and saw Tom leading a team of four horses harnessed to a covered wagon.

"Say how-do to your new mother!" Tom
shouted happily.

Tom helped a woman down from the wagon.
She was tall and had a gentle smile. She came
over to the Lincoln children and put her arms
around them.

"I'm mighty pleased to meet you," Mrs.

Sarah Lincoln said. "Now come and meet my children."

She led Abe, Sarah, and Dennis to the wagon. Standing there were two girls, thirteen-year-old Sarah Elizabeth and ten-year-old Matilda, and one boy, nine-year-old John. Now life at Pigeon Creek wouldn't be lonely anymore. They would be a real family again.

The second Mrs. Lincoln brought many changes to Pigeon Creek. First, she had Abe and John fill a trough with water. Then she bathed Abe and Sarah and told Dennis to scrub himself clean. After that she set about cleaning and washing and dusting the cabin. She had brought good furniture, pewter dishes, feather pillows and mattresses, pots and skillets, a flax wheel, and a soap kettle. All of these were left outside until she felt the house was clean enough for them. She also had Tom put down a wooden floor and build a real door for the cabin. And she had the boys whitewash the walls and ceiling.

37

"Now," she said when everything was done, "we have a proper home!"

Right away, Abe liked his stepmother. She was a kind, intelligent woman, with a good sense of humor. And she brought something with her that interested Abe very much—books. Abe loved to read, and Mrs. Lincoln thought that was just fine.

Tom Lincoln, however, would have liked Abe to forget about "book-learning" and get on with farming. But his wife told him that Abe was going to be a great man someday and should be educated. And so, whenever the school near Pigeon Creek was open, she encouraged Abe to go.

Abe enjoyed school and did his work carefully and well. On one of his arithmetic notebooks, between neat rows of numbers, he wrote:

Abraham Lincoln is my name
And with my pen I wrote the same.
I wrote in both haste and speed
and left it here for fools to read.

The tall, skinny boy practiced writing every chance he got. And he was always reading or getting ready to read. Before setting out to plow the fields in the morning, Abe would put a book inside his shirt and fill his pockets with corn-bread. When noon came, he'd sit down under a tree, reading and eating at the same time. In the house at night, he'd tilt a chair by the chimney and read.

About his passion for reading, Abe himself said, "The things I want to know are in books; my best friend is someone who'll give me a book I haven't read."

There was no library in his part of the world, and very few people owned books. But Abe tracked down the few books there were in that part of Indiana. Once he walked twenty miles to borrow a book about the history of the United States. Another time a neighbor lent him a biography of George Washington. That night, after he finished reading, Abe tucked the book into a corner of the loft. While he slept, there was a big storm, and rain stained the book cover.

To pay for the damage, Abe spent three days harvesting corn for the farmer who had loaned him the book. Even as a youngster, and even when it meant doing hard work, Abe was always truthful and ready to take responsibility for his deeds.

There were two books that meant a lot to the serious teenager. One was an Indiana law book. Abe read it over and over again, until he almost knew it by heart. He wanted to learn everything there was to know about the way laws worked, and how they could be used for the good of people.

Years later, Abe would become a lawyer, even though he didn't go to school for it. He did it by reading every law book he could get his hands on, and working as a clerk for a lawyer in Illinois.

The second book that Abe read over and over had facts about geography, science, and world history. He learned things from this book that his friends and neighbors had never heard of.

Abe *was* different from his friends and neighbors, but he was still well liked. He was a great storyteller, and had a wonderful sense of humor. That was important to people in Pigeon Creek.

Folks used to gather at the village store even when they had nothing to buy. They came to swap tales and gossip. This was one of their favorite ways of entertaining themselves.

Being a good storyteller was a matter of pride, and each person tried to outdo the others. Abe, who had been shy for a long time, "got the hang of talking" in front of the story-swappers at the village store. He learned so well that he was soon the best storyteller for miles around.

That teenage storyteller grew up to become one of the finest public speakers in American history. As a member of the Illinois assembly, as a young lawyer in his famous debates with Stephen Douglas, and as President of the United States, Abe's skill as a speaker won him respect and admiration.

The poor backwoods boy grew up loving people, the land, and the law. One day he would prove his love for all these by serving as his nation's sixteenth president. He would lead his country through the worst days of the Civil War, and give new meaning to the word "liberty."